WITHDRAWN

American Government Today

THE PRESIDENCY

By Mark Sanders

Raintree Steck-Vaughn Publishers

A Harcourt Company

Austin · New York
www.steck-vaughn.com

Published by Raintree Steck-Vaughn Publishers,
an imprint of Steck-Vaughn Company

Library of Congress Cataloging-in-Publication Data
Sanders, Mark C.
    The Presidency / Mark Sanders
        p. cm.—(American government today)
    Includes index.
    ISBN 0-7398-1786-8
        1. President—United States—Juvenile literature. [1. Presidents.]
    I. Title. II. Series.
    JK517.S24 2000
    352.23'0973—dc21   00-030774

Printed in the United States of America
10 9 8 7 6 5 4 3 2 1 W 03 02 01 00

Photo Acknowledgments
P.4 ©AP/Wide World, Inc.; p.10 ©Ruth Fremson/AP/Wide World, Inc.; p.12 ©Greg Gibson/AP/Wide World, Inc.; p.15 ©Joe Marquette/AP/Wide World, Inc.; p.16 ©Ruth Fremson/AP Wide World, Inc.; pp.21, 27 ©AP/Wide World, Inc.; p.33 ©Greg Gibson/AP/Wide World, Inc.; p.34 ©AP/Wide World, Inc.; p.38 ©Peter Lennihan/AP/Wide World, Inc.; p.41 ©AP/Wide World, Inc.

CONTENTS

THE PRESIDENCY

Every four years Americans choose a president, the person they want to lead them. They have done this since 1789, the year George Washington became the first president of the United States. Ever since then, a variety of Americans have served as president. They have come from many states and different backgrounds.

Some of the presidents became great leaders and did important things for the country. Some led the United States through times of difficulties. Others led the country during times of peace and prosperity. All the presidents have helped shape American history in some way.

The person who wins the next presidential election will have many duties. These include carrying out the country's laws, heading the armed forces, and representing the nation in dealings with foreign countries. Today, many people think the president is the most powerful elected official in the world.

The president's office: The Oval Office in the White House, in Washington, D.C.

THE THREE BRANCHES OF THE GOVERNMENT

The founders of the new United States knew that it was not a good idea to have just one person in charge. To keep this from happening, they set up three branches of government. And to make sure that no branch had too much power, the founders created a system of checks and balances.

This means that each branch of the American government can check, or limit, the power of the other two branches because each branch has the power to do only certain things and not others. To get things done, all three branches must work together.

The organization of the U.S. government is written in the document known as the Constitution. It lists all of the written laws that set out the nation's plan of government. It provides general rules that the state and local governments must follow.

The three branches of government set up by the Constitution are the legislative, judicial, and executive branches. Congress is the legislative branch. Article I of the Constitution sets up Congress. It is made up of the Senate and the House of Representatives. The members of Congress make the laws of the country.

The U.S. Constitution

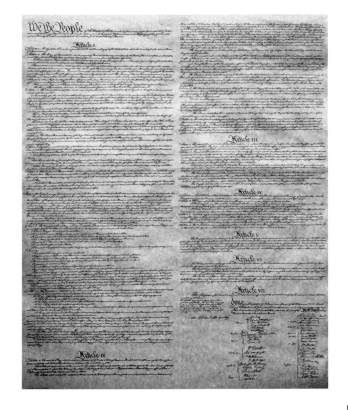

The writers of the Constitution also knew that a judicial branch was needed to interpret the country's laws. The government branch that does this job is the Supreme Court. It was set up in Article III of the Constitution.

Article II of the Constitution sets up how the nation is to be run. The person who heads the government is the president. The president and vice president are elected by the entire country. They are the only government officials who are. The president and the many people who help the president make up the executive branch.

The president heads the executive branch. This branch of government is made up of the Executive Office of the President, 14 executive departments, and more than 100 independent agencies. Today, the executive branch has three million employees and uses more than 500 office buildings in Washington, D.C., alone. These include the Federal Bureau of Investigation (FBI), the National Park Service, and the United States Postal Service.

HOW THE PRESIDENT IS CHOSEN

When the Constitution set up the executive branch of the government, it stated certain things about the presidency. According to the Constitution, a person running for the office of president must meet three conditions. He or she must have been born in the United States. The president must be at least 35 years old. Finally, he or she must have lived in the United States for at least 14 years.

The Constitution states that the president is elected for a term of four years. He or she can then be reelected to serve a second term. A candidate, or the person running for office, becomes president by being elected to the position by the voters of the country. However, if the president dies, resigns, or is removed from office, the vice president becomes president, even though he or she was not actually elected to the office.

A Secret Service agent stands watch during a presidential speaking engagement.

The president and first family are protected by a governmental security group known as the Secret Service. The Secret Service is part of the Department of the Treasury. It belongs to this department because it was originally set up to stop the counterfeiting of money. This means that the job of the Secret Service was to try to keep people from printing false money.

The Secret Service protects the members of the first family wherever they go. This protection continues even after the president has left office. The Secret Service also guards the vice president.

ROLES OF THE PRESIDENT

The Constitution gives the president many specific powers. These are known as formal powers. According to the Constitution, the president is the chief executive. This means that the president runs the country. In this role, one of the president's most important jobs is to carry out the laws that Congress makes.

The president also appoints many government officials, including cabinet members, Supreme Court justices, and other important officials. The Senate must approve these choices.

When there is a national "state of emergency," the president has emergency powers. These powers allow him or her to make certain things happen more quickly. In this sense, the president is "protecting" the Constitution.

President Bill Clinton meets with members of his executive office.

The Constitution also makes the president commander in chief of the armed forces. In this role, the president's main jobs are to defend the United States during a war and to keep it strong during peace.

The president selects all of the top military officers, although Congress has to approve them. The president also determines how big the nation's armed forces should be. Again, Congress must agree.

Only Congress can declare war. Congress has declared "official" wars five times. But over the years presidents have used their powers to send U.S. troops into conflicts even if Congress has not declared war.

**The Senate budget committee meets with the
president's Treasury Secretary and budget advisers.**

Although it is not set out in the Constitution, the
president is also responsible for the budget. A budget is
a plan that tells how much money may be spent. Every
year the president proposes a budget, describing how to
raise and spend money to carry out his or her programs.
But Congress has to approve the budget—and often
makes changes in the process. Taking control of how
much money the United States spends is one of the
president's biggest tasks.

President Clinton, in his role as chief diplomat for the United States, shakes hands with Palestinian President Yasser Arafat.

The president may also suggest laws for Congress to pass. Each January the president delivers a "State of the Union" message to Congress. This speech reviews the country's successes and lists its major problems. At the same time, it outlines the president's goals and programs he or she thinks will solve the problems. The speech also tells Congress what new laws the president will suggest during the coming year. The president and his or her advisers may even draft, or prepare, such laws for Congress to pass.

Once a bill, or a law that has been proposed, has been approved by Congress, the president receives it to sign. The president may veto the bill. This means that the president refuses to pass the bill into law. Being able to veto a bill is an important presidential power. However, if two-thirds of both houses of Congress pass the bill again, they can override, or set aside, the president's veto. This means the bill can still become a law over the president's veto.

The president is also chief diplomat of the United States. This means he or she represents the nation in dealings with foreign countries. The Constitution gives the president the power to appoint ambassadors, or U.S. officials who represent the government in foreign countries, with the approval of Congress.

The president also plays a major role in making foreign policy. These are plans for how the United States should act toward other countries.

As chief diplomat, the president may make treaties, or formal agreements, with other countries. But each treaty needs a two-thirds approval from Congress. On the other hand, the president does not need the approval of Congress to make executive agreements, which are like treaties.

As chief of state, the president attends different ceremonies. For instance, he or she goes to historical celebrations and the openings of new buildings. The president also presents awards to people who have done something very brave or special.

Some of these events may seem unimportant. But they bring the president closer to the people. This is important because the president is also a communicator. The leader of the world's most powerful democracy has to understand the citizens of the United States. He or she must get them to work together for the good of the country.

The president has formal powers that are stated in the Constitution. In addition, the president has other kind of powers called inherent powers. These powers are based on the president's interpretation of what can

and cannot be done. The president's inherent powers
are the result of what previous presidents have done
over the nation's past 200-plus years.

Presidents have claimed the right to some other
powers. One of them is "executive privilege."
Executive privilege allows the president to keep certain
information secret from Congress and courts.

The country's first three presidents were George
Washington, John Adams, and Thomas Jefferson. They
were the first to claim special executive privilege.

**Thomas Jefferson, the third president of
the United States**

THE VICE PRESIDENT

The vice president is second in command after the president. If the president is unable to serve in office, the vice president takes over as president. The vice president must be ready to take over as president the moment it becomes necessary. This is set out in the Constitution. If the vice president cannot serve, the Speaker of the House of Representatives is next in line to become president.

One of the vice president's main jobs is to serve as head of the U.S. Senate. This, too, is set out in the Constitution. In this role, the vice president is in charge of Senate sessions. However, the vice president cannot take part in debates and can vote only in the event of a tie in a Senate vote.

Other than this responsibility, the vice president's role in the U.S. government may not be large. That is because the Constitution does not give the vice president any other official duties. As such, the vice president is only as strong as the powers he or she is given by the president.

The vice president is selected at the same national convention as the presidential candidate. There may be several reasons why he or she was chosen. The president may have wanted this person as vice president. Or he or she may have been one of the losing candidates for president. As well, the vice presidential choice may be from a state with many voters. Or else this person was chosen to run because he or she is the opposite of the president. By running together, the two candidates hope to make as many voters as possible happy.

Vice president Al Gore (left) listens and gives advice during a Cabinet meeting.

THE OVAL OFFICE

Since 1800, every president and first family has lived in the White House, in Washington, D.C., while the president is in office. Recent presidents have also had a home at Camp David, in the mountains of Maryland.

The president doesn't just live in the White House. He or she also does much work there, in the Oval Office. The president's office is located in the southwest corner of the West Wing. Meeting rooms and other offices surround the Oval Office. The same room has been used since 1934. Before that time, the president's office was in another oval-shaped room. This office was in the part of the building where the president's family lives on an upper floor in the White House.

Some 400 people work in the White House itself. These are mostly members of the Executive Office of the President. These people help and advise the president. Many more staff members work a short distance away, in a building known as the Old Executive Office Building.

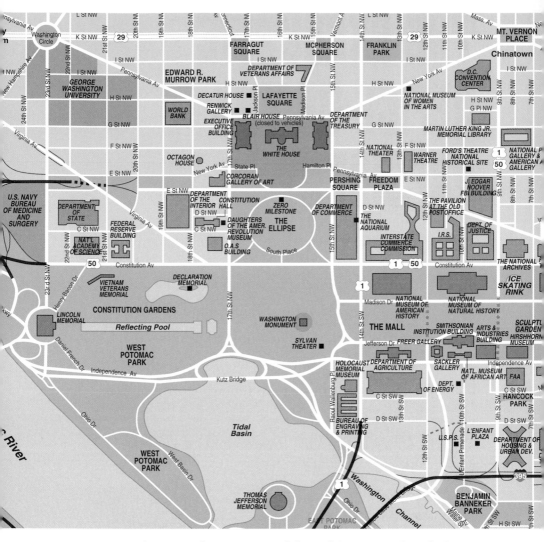

A map showing the position of the White House in relation
to the rest of Washinton, D.C.

THE EXECUTIVE OFFICE OF THE PRESIDENT

One section of the executive branch of the government is the Executive Office of the President. It is made up of a number of government agencies that offer the president advice on foreign issues and ones in the United States. Following are the agencies that make up the Executive Office.

The Office of the Vice President belongs to the Executive Office. The White House Office is another part of it. The White House Office is composed of the president's closest personal advisers. These people advise him or her on all matters of policy and on how to deal with Congress and the media, or press.

The chief of staff heads the White House Office. This person decides who may or may not see the president. He or she may also fire employees if they are not doing a good job. For this reason, the chief of staff is not always popular.

Another member of the White House Office is the president's special counsel. The special counsel works to make sure that actions taken by the president are legal.

The president's press secretary handles public appearances and press conferences. The president regularly meets with newspaper reporters and television reporters during these press conferences. Often he or she is the spokesperson for the president in situations where the president does not appear.

Members of the White House Office are appointed by the president without the need for the Senate's approval. When the current president leaves office, these people will be replaced.

The agencies listed on page 26 are also part of the Executive Office of the President. However, while the heads of these agencies are appointed by the president, the Senate must approve of the choices.

THE EXECUTIVE OFFICE

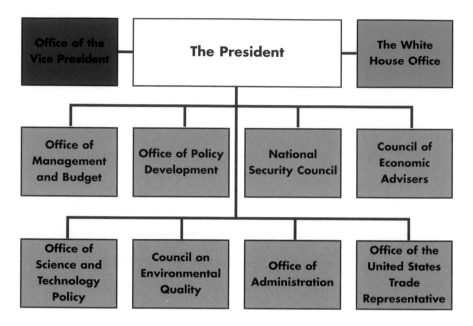

One of the most important agencies of the Executive Office is the National Security Council (NSC). It oversees the agency that gathers information about foreign nations as well as the country's defense agency.

Another major branch is the Office of Management and Budget (OMB). This office prepares the yearly national budget that the president submits to Congress.

There are six smaller but still important agencies. The Office of Policy Development is in charge of decisions that affect the country's direction. The Council of Economic Advisers stays aware of and reports on the nation's economy. The Office of Science and Technology Policy is concerned with such items as space travel, new trends in science, and alternate energy sources. The Council on Environmental Quality's main concern is just that: the environment. The Office of the United States Trade Representative is concerned with foreign trade policy and how it should be handled. Finally, the Office of Administration assists each part of the Executive Office.

President Clinton and members of the National Security Council meeting in the Oval Office in 1994

THE EXECUTIVE DEPARTMENTS

Another section of the executive branch of the government is the executive departments. These departments manage the federal government. The following list gives the executive departments.

Department of State This is one of the oldest departments, dating back to 1789. It directs relations with all foreign countries. This department carries out foreign policy, including setting up treaties.

Department of the Treasury Also established in 1789, the Treasury deals with matters about money. Agencies within this department collect federal taxes, mint coins, and print postage stamps and paper money. The Department of the Treasury tries to catch counterfeiters, who try to make and circulate false money.

Department of Defense This branch maintains the country's military forces, including the Army, the Navy, the Marine Corps, and the Air Force. The Department of Defense is located in the Pentagon. This is a large governemtn office building near Washington, D.C. Defense is the largest of the executive departments.

Department of Justice This department runs the Federal Bureau of Investigation (FBI) and represents the country in all legal matters.

Department of Agriculture This agency looks after farm programs. It provides cash payments to help farmers in their work. The Department of Agriculture has hundreds of agents. They inspect agricultural products for quality.

Department of Commerce This department aids businesses and conducts the U.S. Census every ten years. A census is an official count of all the people in the country.

Department of Education This department takes care of the federal government's education programs. It checks the progress of education around the country. In addition, it prepares guidelines for giving tax money to school districts.

Department of Energy This office deals with energy policy and research. Agencies for energy resources, such as coal, oil, and atomic energy, are part of this department.

Department of Health and Human Services After the Department of Defense, this is the nation's largest agency. Its work affects more American citizens than any other department. Among its responsibilities are running the Social Security system (and issuing monthly social security checks), handing out food stamps, and payments for health care.

Department of Housing and Urban Development This department takes care of all federal housing and urban developments. It also works to improve housing.

Department of the Interior This office manages the nation's resources, including public lands, wildlife, national parks, and historic sites.

Department of Labor Unemployment Minimum wage laws are just some of the things this department deals with. It also fights age, gender, and racial inequality in the workplace.

Department of Transportation This group is responsible for all national highway and mass transportation programs, including railroads and airlines.

Department of Veterans Affairs This department was designed to help people who have served in the armed forces. The department takes care of medical services for former soldiers, payments, and health care, among other things.

The head of each executive department is appointed by the president with the approval of the Senate. The heads of all the departments except one are called secretaries. Only the head of the Department of Justice is not. He or she is called the attorney general.

Today, the heads of the 14 executive departments make up an important group of advisers to the president, called the cabinet. The secretary of state is the highest ranking member of the cabinet.

The Constitution says nothing about the cabinet. However, George Washington began the practice of informally consulting with the heads of his departments.

The president meets regularly with the cabinet. Together they discuss progress in all areas of public life. However, although cabinet members offer their opinions and suggestions on issues and policies, a decision is never put to a vote. The president alone makes the decisions. That is his or her responsibility, and no one else's.

Cabinet members stand and applaud during the president's "State of the Union" address.

INDEPENDENT AGENCIES

The executive branch of the government also includes many separate agencies. Some of these agencies are controlled by the executive departments, but many of them are independent. This means, they have been set up to run completely on their own. Some of the best known are shown in the list on page 35.

EPA members meet in Illinois to discuss agricultural concerns.

Central Intelligence Agency (CIA)
Collects information about other nations to help the United States protect itself. Part of the National Security Council.

Commission on Civil Rights Enforces civil rights laws, which protect the personal rights of U.S. citizens.

Environmental Protection Agency (EPA) Enforces laws to protect the nation's air, land, and water.

Federal Deposit Insurance Corporation (FDIC) Provides protection for many kinds of money that people have in banks.

National Aeronautics and Space Administration (NASA) Operates the nation's space programs.

Peace Corps Sends volunteers to many countries to help the people who live there.

IMPEACHMENT

The U.S. Constitution says that the president, vice president, and all civil officers can be "removed from office on impeachment for, and conviction of, treason, bribery, or other high crimes and misdemeanors." To impeach means to formally accuse a government official of wrongdoing. Impeachment is a strong form of accusation. Only twice has the impeachment process been used against a president. And in neither case was the president removed from office.

According to the Constitution, only the House of Representatives can begin and end the impeachment process. If two-thirds of the House members vote for impeachment, then there is a trial in the Senate. The Senate serves as the jury. If found guilty by a two-thirds vote, the official is then removed from office.

In 1868, the House of Representatives voted to impeach President Andrew Johnson for violating, among other things, the Tenure of Office Act. This act said that the president could not fire a federal official who had been approved by the Senate.

Johnson believed the Tenure of Office Act was unconstitutional. This means that it goes against the Constitution. He removed Secretary of War Edwin M. Stanton from office. The impeached Johnson was tried by the Senate. However, he was found not guilty by one vote.

More recently, the impeachment of President Bill Clinton divided the nation. Perjury, or telling a lie under oath, was one of the charges. In December 1998, the House found Clinton guilty of two of four impeachment charges. These were lying under oath, or perjury, and obstructing, or harming, justice.

In fact Clinton's impeachment was largely a battle of party issues. Republican members of Congress wanted to discredit the president, a Democrat. And Democrats, not surprisingly, supported him.

In February 1999 the impeachment trial came before the Senate. There again, Republicans voted against Clinton, and Democrats supported him. The Senate could not get the two-thirds vote needed to remove the president from office. All 45 Democratic senators voted to acquit Clinton, or find him not guilty of the charges, and a major government crisis was narrowly avoided. The government, and the office of the president, remained secure.

In 1974, President Richard M. Nixon was accused of trying to cover up a break-in at the Democratic National Committee headquarters in the Watergate building in Washington, D.C. Members of the White House staff helped plan the break-in and later tried to cover up the crime. Several of them were tried and sent to prison.

A Senate committee looking into the case found that President Nixon had taped all his White House conversations. The committee asked for the tapes because they might have important information. Nixon refused to hand over these tapes, claiming executive privilege. The case was reviewed by the Supreme Court. The justices ordered Nixon to hand over the tapes. The tapes clearly showed Nixon's guilt. Rather than face impeachment, Nixon resigned from the presidency on August 9, 1974.

Bill Clinton's impeachment in 1998 made headlines all over the United States.

THE CHANGING PRESIDENCY

Much of the excitement of each president's term in office has come from the ways in which the president has done things differently. The president's personality has always been important. After Washington, Adams, and Jefferson, Andrew Jackson was one of the most colorful of the early presidents. Some referred to him as "King Andrew."

Later, Abraham Lincoln's handling of the Civil War and ending of slavery in the Confederate states helped make him a great president.

At the beginning of the 20th century presidents began to have a consistently strong presence. The country was becoming a major power and the president became a world figure. Theodore Roosevelt was a very visible president. He was loud and forceful. He had

A gathering of 20th-century presidents and their wives. From left, Bill Clinton and Hillary Rodham Clinton; George and Barbara Bush; Ronald and Nancy Reagan; Jimmy and Rosalyn Carter; Gerald and Betty Ford.

young children, whose behavior amused the nation. Roosevelt's personality helped make him a powerful national leader.

His cousin, Franklin D. Roosevelt, became president 30 years later, in 1933. Roosevelt was the first president to address the nation over the radio. His weekly radio talks became famous, and people all over the country were eager to hear him speak.

Franklin D. Roosevelt took office in the midst of one of the nation's worst crises: the Great Depression. The stock market had crashed. Banks failed. Many people were out of work. Roosevelt created jobs to put people back to work. From his policies grew many of the agencies and departments that are still part of the government today.

Then World War II began in Europe in 1939. And in 1941, the Japanese bombed the American fleet at Pearl Harbor, Hawaii, and the United States entered the war.

Since the end of World War II in 1945, most presidents have been well known all over the world. In 1960 John F. Kennedy promised a new kind of politics. He was killed just three years after he became president. Lyndon B. Johnson and Richard M. Nixon followed Kennedy. Since then, Ronald Reagan, George Bush, and Bill Clinton have been popular presidents.

U.S. PRESIDENTS AND VICE PRESIDENTS

George Washington (1789-1797)
VP John Adams (1789-1797)

John Adams (1797-1801)
VP Thomas Jefferson (1797-1801)

Thomas Jefferson (1801-1809)
VP Aaron Burr (1801-1805)
VP George Clinton (1805-1809)

James Madison (1809-1817)
VP George Clinton (1809-1812)
VP Elbridge Gerry (1813-1814)

James Monroe (1817-1825)
VP Daniel D. Tompkins (1817-1825)

John Quincy Adams (1825-1829)
VP John C. Calhoun (1825-1829)

Andrew Jackson (1829-1837)
VP John C. Calhoun (1829-1832)
VP Martin Van Buren (1833-1837)

P **Martin Van Buren (1837-1841)**
VP Richard M. Johnson (1837-1841)

P **William Henry Harrison (1841)**
VP John Tyler (1841)

P **John Tyler (1841-1845)**
no vice president

P **James K. Polk (1845-1849)**
VP George M. Dallas (1845-1849)

Zachary Taylor (1849-1850)
VP Millard Fillmore (1849-1850)

Millard Fillmore (1850-1853)
no vice president

Franklin Pierce (1853-1857)
VP William R. King (1853)

James Buchanan (1857-1861)
VP John C. Breckinridge (1857-1861)

Abraham Lincoln (1861-1865)
VP Hannibal Hamlin (1861-1865)
VP Andrew Johnson (1865)

Andrew Johnson (1865-1869)
no vice president

Ulysses S. Grant (1869-1877)
VP Schuyler Colfax (1869-1873)
VP Henry Wilson (1873-1875)

43

P **Rutherford B. Hayes (1877-1881)**
VP William A. Wheeler (1877-1881)

P **James A. Garfield (1881)**
VP Chester A. Arthur (1881)

P **Chester A. Arthur (1881-1885)**
no vice president

P **Grover Cleveland (1885-1889)**
VP Thomas A. Hendricks (1885)

P **Benjamin Harrison (1889-1893)**
VP Levi P. Morton (1889-1893)

P **Grover Cleveland (1893-1897)**
VP Adlai E. Stevenson (1893-1897)

P **William McKinley (1897-1901)**
VP Garret A. Hobart (1897-1899)
VP Theodore Roosevelt (1901)

P **Theodore Roosevelt (1901-1909)**
VP Charles W. Fairbanks (1905-1909)

P **William H. Taft (1909-1913)**
VP James S. Sherman (1909-1912)

P **Woodrow Wilson (1913-1921)**
VP Thomas R. Marshall (1913-1921)

P **Warren G. Harding (1921-1923)**
VP Calvin Coolidge (1921-1923)

P **Calvin Coolidge (1923-1929)**
VP Charles G. Dawes (1925-1929)

P **Herbert Hoover (1929-1933)**
VP Charles Curtis (1929-1933)

P **Franklin D. Roosevelt (1933-1945)**
VP John N. Garner (1933-1941)
VP Henry A. Wallace (1941-1945)
VP Harry S. Truman (1945)

P **Harry S. Truman (1945-1953)**
VP Alben W. Barkley (1949-1953)

P **Dwight D. Eisenhower (1953-1961)**
VP Richard Nixon (1953-1961)

P **John F. Kennedy (1961-1963)**
VP Lyndon B. Johnson (1961-1963)

P **Lyndon B. Johnson (1963-1969)**
VP Hubert Humphrey (1965-1969)

P **Richard Nixon (1969-1974)**
VP Spiro T. Agnew (1969-1973)
VP Gerald Ford (1973-1974)

P **Gerald Ford (1974-1977)**
VP Nelson A. Rockefeller (1974-1977)

P **James Carter (1977-1981)**
VP Walter Mondale (1977-1981)

P **Ronald Reagan (1981-1989)**
VP George Bush (1981-1989)

P **George Bush (1989-1993)**
VP J. Danforth Quayle (1989-1993)

P **William Clinton (1993-2001)**
VP Albert Gore (1993-2001)

GLOSSARY

Cabinet A group of people who advise the president; made up of executive department heads

Candidate A person running for office

Constitution Written laws that set out the nation's plan of government. It provides general rules that the state and local governments must follow.

Emergency powers Powers a president has during a national "state of emergency" that allow him or her to make certain things happen more quickly

Executive branch The part of the U.S. government that decides how to carry out laws. It is headed by the president.

Executive departments The government departments that manage the federal government

Executive Office of the President The government agencies that work directly for the president, offering him or her advice on foreign and domestic issues

Executive privilege The right of the president to keep information secret from Congress and the courts

Impeachment Trying a public official because of wrongdoing

Independent agencies Government agencies that oversee federal programs in many fields. Some of these agencies are controlled by the executive departments, while others operate independently

Judicial branch The part of the government that explains and interprets the laws of the country. It is headed by the Supreme Court.

Legislative branch The part of the government that makes the laws of the country. It is known as Congress and is made up of the Senate and the House of Representatives.

Oval Office The room in which the president works while at the White House in Washington, D.C.

President The person the voters of a country elect to lead them

Treaty Formal agreements with other countries that need the approval of the Senate

Veto To reject a bill

Vice president The elected official who becomes president in the event the president dies, resigns, or is removed from office

White House Office The agency made up of the president's closest personal advisers

INDEX